GW01072110

90 Days

Unlocking Your Financial Freedom to Change Your Life Forever

NICOLE DEAS

© 2020 Nicole Deas. All Rights Reserved.

All rights reserved. No part of this publication may be reproduced or transmitted in any form or by any means, electronic or mechanical, including photocopy, recording, or information storage and retrieval system, without the written permission of the author.

Cover: Christian Cuan
Edited & Formatting: U Can Mark My Word Editorial Services
Gold Chain Cover Designed by Macrovector/Freepik

Published in the United States of America by Nicole Deas, Inc.
Acworth, Georgia, in 2019.

Second Edition Published by Pen Legacy Publishing in 2020

For author appearance inquiries and interviews, contact the author via email at ndeas@nicoledeas.com

Library of Congress Cataloging in Publication Data

ISBN: 978-1-7348278-8-0

Dedication

This book is dedicated to every person, young and old, employed and unemployed, educated and uneducated, that dreams of becoming financially independent and building a happy, successful, and rewarding life but is too intimidated to take that first step.

It is my hope and dream that this book might be that first step.

Thank You!

…to my grandmother, mother, and sister who modeled behavior that helped to shape the woman I am today!

…to my husband, Darrin – it's a privilege to share my business, life, and love with you.

…to my children, Imani and Kanye – your growth provides a constant source of joy, pride, and inspiration.

TABLE OF CONTENTS

Who Am I to Be Writing This Book?

I know you have probably read countless books and listened to tons of financial coaches, advisors, and pretenders who explain why you should get your finances in order. So, I am not going to pretend as if I have all the answers and can solve every problem. However, I would be doing you an injustice if I offered no advice. Although you may not agree with my mindset regarding money, I learned from my debt, countless collection calls, low credit scores, and rejection letters just how important it is to have good credit.

While growing up in a single-family, first-generation household, my sister and I were taught that money is essential. It is the foundation of a healthy wealth strategy. We were told that credit should only be used when necessary, not for impulsive purchases. Now remember, back in the '70s, there was no abundance of store credit cards. My mother had American Express and Macy's credit cards. That was it. Back then, my sister and I had no idea what a credit card even was because we would wait off to the side while my mother stood in line to pay. We had no clue what things costs or if she paid with cash, check, or credit.

My sister and I watched our mom budget; we observed her divvy cash into envelopes for the month. At the time, I had no idea that was called the "envelope method". She used the money to pay for whatever she had written on the envelope, and when the cash ran out, that was it—no more spending. We were taught to save money, budget it, pay what we owed, and not squander it.

At this juncture, I need you to know that my mother and father are immigrants from Trinidad and Panama, respectively. They came to America for the same reason so many other immigrants do—to have a better life. My mother was nineteen years old, and my father was twenty when they arrived in New York City. Both settled in Brooklyn, where they met a few years later. Upon arriving in America, my mother, who was a high school graduate and wanted to become a nurse, cleaned homes of families. She worked during the day and went to school at night. Somehow during those long hours, she found time to court my father, get married, and have two daughters. By the time she finished going to school, she had a bachelor's degree, master's degree, and nursing degree—all with no debt. My sister and I did not want for anything. We were well-fed, the utilities never got disconnected, and we went on vacation every summer to visit our family in Trinidad. I thought my childhood was like every other child's, but apparently, it was not. We lived in a two-family home that my mother owned, and my grandmother lived five miles away in her own home. My aunt and uncle, who lived a few miles away, owned their home, as well. So, it should come as no surprise that I grew up understanding the value of homeownership.

Now, just because I grew up with this background, I still had my hang-ups about money. When I got my first job at Citibank, N.A. on 59th Street as a junior in high school, I knew how to deposit my check, which I did religiously. It was not because I understood the benefits of saving, but because my mother checked my bank book to make sure I did it. This was before the time of online banking. Back then, banks closed at 3:00 p.m. during the week, and you had to visit the bank to conduct your business. I had a savings account and a checking account but no bank card because they weren't available in the '80s. When I cashed my check, I took out about forty dollars, which lasted until the next payday. Since I had a bus pass provided to me by the school, I did not have to pay to ride the bus or train to school and work, which made it a bit easier to stretch my money until I got paid again.

However, during my senior year, I developed an intense love for sneakers. Especially Reeboks. I had every color! Instead of just taking out forty dollars, it turned into eighty dollars. I'm sure my mother noticed the increase in the amount I was withdrawing, but she did not say anything. Well, not until my bank account balance started to take a dive. Instead of depositing my paycheck, I would cash the check and walk around with all that money. It was my money that I had earned by working, so why not? Most teenagers feel they can handle their finances. How quickly I would learn that age does not determine one's ability to be responsible.

During the last semester of my senior year, my mother told me that the fees for my senior dues and the senior trip to the Bahamas would be my responsibility. She said since I had been working and per her calculations, I should be able to handle paying for the airfare and my class ring, which totaled $490.00. By this time, my bank balance was less than two hundred dollars. That was my first lesson of savings versus spending and the reality of both. Saving so I can spend later is a topic that turned into a frequent conversation between my mother and me.

I do not want to mislead you to believe I have not had pitfalls in my forty-eight years of living. Honestly, I have had quite a few. But, from each one, I learned not to make the same mistake again. In my early 20s, I learned the importance of credit. Back when I was growing up, credit scores were not readily available on an app. The only time you found out your score is if you were going through the process of buying a car or house.

I found out at the age of twenty-three how important credit scores were when I had to purchase my first car. My 1987 Nissan Stanza had been with me throughout college, a drive to Georgia after I graduated from college, and during my first couple of years as an independent young adult. But, when I woke up to go to work one day, the car wouldn't start. The alternator had gone bad. Well, to fix my vehicle would set me back over $1,200.00. I had nowhere near that amount in my checking or savings account, and back then, Firestone and NTB did not offer store credit cards. So, I thought to myself that I would purchase a new car. Humph! Not with my credit. The Honda dealership I visited did not like what they saw on my credit report. You see, there is this thing called collections, and because of my college debt and having a history of late payments, my credit score was not desirable. How dare they deny me a car!

With the realization that I was not perfect, I knew I had to get this together. After walking and taking the bus in Cobb County, Georgia (my GA folks know that was no fun), I got my whole self together. I stopped feeling down about my situation and got a second job at Express. I paid off the collections and paid down all of my credit cards, which totaled about $3,000. I saved $5,000 up and lived on a salary of $15,000, even though my actual salary was $45K. My mother always said to live below your means and SAVE. Real-life had hit me.

I always liked how money worked but more in the way of the stock market and investments. I never really thought of credit and debt playing a part in how money worked. I was young back then but learned quickly that the two are inextricably linked. Thus, Nicole Deas, the Wealth Strategist, was born.

Are You Ready to Be Re-Educated on Money?

"The secret to wealth is simple: Find a way to do more for others than anyone else does. Become more valuable. Do more. Give more. Be more. Serve more."

~ Tony Robbins

Money Master the Game: 7 Simple Steps to Financial Freedom

Every financial planning session with a new client begins the same way: *So, tell me about your childhood.* I have been in this business long enough to expect confused, blank stares in response to my request. As a successful man or woman struggles to understand the purpose of the inquiry, they slowly gather themselves and give half-hearted, polite answers. I need to press deeper to understand the WHY. We are all products of our past and can attest to the role of childhood experiences in shaping our adult experiences and financial futures. In the conversation that follows, values begin to emerge, values that shape how clients live and how they spend money.

My mother was a woman who was *careful with money*. Our cupboards and refrigerator were well stocked with various snacks—cakes, cookies, ice cream, and popcorn. When our friends lined up at the truck to buy Mister Softee ice cream (the 1978 equivalent of Coldstone Creamery) in the summer, we headed toward our refrigerator for our goodies. Mommy did not believe in buying name brand shoes or clothing. She would often tell us it was the fit that counts, not the labels. She would jokingly tell us if we needed to wear name brands that badly, she would embroider our names on our clothing. Needless to say, as kids, we did not find that funny.

When it came to money, my mother taught us well. We were children who didn't find satisfaction in frivolous items. Our house was not based on an expectation of excess. My mother bought what was needed, not what we wanted at the moment. It may sound rigid, but our family was filled with love. We simply lived by more wholesome standards. It may not be the typical childhood story for some who read this book, but it may resonate with others. Children are shaped to expect things that they may never earn. I consider myself lucky to have been taught lessons about spending.

Commercial media tempts us in the middle of our favorite shows. Advertisements lead us to believe our car will elevate our confidence and social status. Social media is our marketing tool to demonstrate to everyone the best snapshot seconds of our normal snapshot lives. However, a simple glance at our national financial status shows that we are far from where we should be.

In a 2018 report on the well-being of American households, the following are the statistics on emergency spending:

- Four in ten adults, if faced with an unexpected expense of $400, would be unable to cover it or would cover it by selling something or borrowing money. This is an improvement from half of the adults in 2013 being ill-prepared for such an expense.
- Over one-fifth of adults are not able to pay all of their current month's bills in full.
- Over one-fourth of adults skipped necessary medical care in 2017 due to being unable to afford the cost.

The Federal Reserve Report is simply one in a myriad of reports and data points. Nevertheless, these reports only represent a portion of the financial picture. Something is hiding in plain sight behind every purchase we make, and that is acceptance. As jarring as it may be for you, relationships and social status drive our financial decision-making.

After I shock my clients with the conversation about their childhood, we take an honest assessment of their financial status. Most will admit they are not where they should or want to be. An evaluation of their spending habits reveals the deeper story, which is most spend their money on wants and not needs. Most of us desire financial freedom, but we live in a society that makes us believe others will value us more if we drive a Mercedes-Benz instead of a Honda. It would be frowned upon to walk into a room wearing last year's fashion. *Consumerism tries to conquer us.* The desire for more has consumed us. Corporations have become the gatekeepers of social acceptance by creating a correlation between products and personal fulfillment. Now don't get me wrong, I am all for spending money on nice things *within your budget,* but do you know *why* you are spending?

As you have probably guessed, this is not an *ordinary*

financial-help book. We will not talk extensively about the small details of how money works because that would bore you to tears. This is a book for financial education. However, before you can be successful with your financial literacy, you must change your mindset. I firmly believe financial responsibility is a matter of self-esteem. Your annual salary is not as crucial to your financial success as your self-belief. You must rise above what you think other people are looking at and get to the heart of what creates financial freedom for you.

If you discovered you had 90 days left to live, what would you do? Who would you do it with, and why? We will take a deeper dive into what this would look like for you later. I do not believe a catastrophic diagnosis is necessary for you to live the life you have always wanted. By stepping out of the rat race and shifting your mindset, you can achieve the financial freedom you have always desired, and it can be forever. But you must change. You must unplug, and you must shift. Shift into the reality of what every day of the rest of your life can be. It is time. Forever starts now…

What is Money?

"Money is only a tool. It will take you wherever you wish, but it will not replace you as the driver."

~ Ayn Rand

Recently, I took some vacation time in Florida. I used to travel to places with a plethora of attractions and activities in my younger years, but now, I enjoy going to the beach. As a working wife and mother, there is nothing more refreshing than sliding my feet into the warm sand and reclining with my favorite drink of choice. When the sun embraces my skin and the slight ocean breeze whips around me, I feel as though I am in heaven. I feel relaxed and calm with my husband, children, or friends around, soaking in every moment of bliss. From sights and scenery, to smells and sounds, I love being near the water. During our vacation, we talk, smile, laugh, and share our dreams. The part I liked best about vacationing was having my phone OFF. A few people knew how to reach us, but we spent most of our time without any contact with the outside world. Having a very demanding job, this is a rare luxury for me. I can easily work up to sixty hours a week during busy seasons, with everyone expecting me to be attentive to my profession's various needs. As much as I love my work, I find that I work hardest when those beach moments are approaching. Most admittedly, the moments at the beach represent financial freedom for my family and me.

What is money? When someone asks me that question, I like to tell them about my vacations. I tell them just how much I enjoy spending time with my family on a beach. I do this because you cannot define money without discussing its purpose. Everyone has different goals that they have set for their financial freedom. As I always say, financial freedom is what you define it to be for you. For some, it is the beach experience. For others, it is traveling, going on adventures, and or hobbies that fulfill you. Whatever your need for money is, it represents your financial freedom. As you begin your economic transformation, realize that the purpose of money is to achieve financial freedom. How much you own or the name brands that adorn your body do not define money. Money is defined by you and used to get you to your place of financial freedom. Money is ultimately a tool.

The purpose of money is to help us define how we spend our time. Financial freedom is being able to make choices about our time without being constrained by a lack of money. Poverty restricts, but wealth liberates. In our capitalistic society, money is the mechanism by which you acquire the power to make personal choices. This fact may be a mentality shift for you to digest, and if it is, I am not surprised.

As I define money, I also seek to explain what money is not. Despite what you may have heard from people in the church who wag their judgmental fingers in your face, money is not the root of all evil. Money is not something to be afraid of or run from in fear of what it will do to your life. Contrary to popular belief, money does not change you. Money shows the true character of the person who possesses it. It has no corrosive power of its own, but it can expose many things. Money is also not time. The clichéd expression "time is money" may sound good to us, but it is woefully inaccurate. Time is time, and money is money. The two can fuel each other, but they are not equal. For me, as I explain in the vacation story, money is a quality of life and has been connected to one's quality of life for centuries.

History tells us that ancient Inca tribes created the largest and wealthiest empire in South America without any monetary concept. In other words, they had no currency. Their famous contemporaries, the Aztecs and Mayans, used a system of bartering and trading goods to buy and sell products, but the Incas were unique. Through a complex system known as Mit'a, every Incan male was required by their laws to provide labor to their country for a specific number of days, sometimes upwards of two-thirds of the year. During their time of labor, they built the country from the ground up. From functional buildings to elaborate royal palaces, everything that archaeologists recognize about this ancient tribe was built using this system. Instead of paying the males to get whatever they needed from the marketplace, the government provided all the necessities. Everything from food and clothes, to housing and tools were given to the workers by the rulers in exchange for their allotted days of work. Imagine this; there were no shops, no markets, no malls, and therefore, no money. In their system of value, they saw no need for it. Even in their day, money was simply a tool—a tool this civilization deemed unnecessary.

Our American system of money has more complicated origins. Established in 1690, when the first explorers arrived on the beaches of the New World, our country issued money to pay for military exploits that the colonies promised were backed by precious metals, like gold and silver. Despite the government's claims, the people eventually discovered that they were unable to redeem the paper currency, and the money quickly lost its value. This changed in the year 1775 with the Continental Congress, when money was officially printed as currency. While these early bills were easily counterfeited and subjected to inflation, they were something people could use for purchases. With the signing of the National Banking Act during the Civil War, the dollar became the official American currency. After President Lincoln signed these bills into law, the United States had its first uniform currency. Without boring you with a complete history of our currency ups and downs, I can tell you that from the early settlers in the New World to the tragic Great Depression in the 20th century, to the economic expansion of the 1990s, American money is deeply connected with American emotions. The value of money and Wall Street is all about what we think.

Do you know the actual value of the items you are purchasing? In 2016, a sneaker review website released some jaw-dropping information regarding the true production costs of some popular shoes. The study of the production of Nike, Asics, and Adidas revealed a wide disparity between how much the company spends making the shoe and how much the consumer spends purchasing them.

Pay attention, parents. The Nike Free Flyknits cost $130 on the market, yet only cost $26 to produce. Similarly, the Nike Free RN's cost $100 for consumers while only costing the company $18 to produce. Adidas' Yeezy Boost 750s, designed by hip-hop mogul Kanye West, were made with quality materials costing $76 but were still sold for an astounding $350. Most shockingly, the coveted Nike Air Max 2016's cost the company $33 to make, but they were sold for $190, representing a 600% markup. The average Jordan sneaker, under the best-selling shoe brand Nike, cost the company $16 to make, while consumers pay $250-$300 for a new pair. Essentially, each time you purchase a new shoe at full price, you are paying for the company's marketing campaigns. Think about this information the next time you spend money on a tennis shoe that costs $20 but has been marked up because of the logo.

Shoes, technology, and clothing mark-ups represent a fundamental issue with our current understanding of financial wealth. We spend to make ourselves feel better or to escape feeling sad, depressed, or hurt. From the earliest days of advanced civilization to our smartphone generation, we spend money on things that can satisfy our emotional needs. In a society held captive by consumerism, everyone needs an anchor to ensure they are using money according to its purpose and not falling into the societal trap of emotional spending.

If you discovered you had 90 days left to live, what would you do? It can be anything from going to a game to watch your favorite athlete play, taking a trip around the world, visiting your favorite restaurants, or jumping out of an airplane. My guess is you will not be preoccupied with shoes, clothes, or gadgets, and that is the point. Life looks different when we sit down to define what we value and what is most important to us.

Think about the question and write your answers in the space provided. With each answer, be sure to include who you want to do it with and a brief description of why. I only have one requirement: Do not hold back. Do not limit yourself about what you could or could not do in the timeframe. Dream as big as your imagination.

THE LESSON

Money is a tool to influence our quality of life and financial freedom. If we honor the true value of money and its ability to impact our financial freedom, we can live comfortably and possibly be wealthy. To do so requires dedication and determination to change our relationship with things and money.

Make the "Sit-Down"

"A journey of a thousand miles must begin with a single step."
~ Lao Tzu

One of my favorite stories in biblical scriptures is the story of Jesus feeding the five thousand people who came to hear Him speak. As with all Bible stories, there is usually a valuable lesson that can be perceived differently. According to the story, Jesus began to teach the people profound life principles, and just like many modern-day preachers, He went a bit over time. The Bible says the day was now far spent, which is a polite way of saying He had been long-winded, and everyone was now hungry. After His disciples (or personal assistants) informed Him of the time, they encouraged

Him to release the people so they could go and satisfy their hunger. But Jesus, who was compassionate, decided to perform a beautiful demonstration instead. He miraculously turned a young boy's lunch of five loaves and two fish into a meal that fed thousands of people. Everyone left with full bellies and to-go plates for later. Before performing the miracle, Jesus made a statement most people miss. He instructed his assistants to make them sit down. Before they could experience this blessing, they had to stop and focus.

Whether or not you are religious, I hope you can appreciate the principle of this action. With just a few words, the great teacher modeled a key principle for accomplishing your 90-day journey. Before you can experience wealth and abundance, you must sit down and organize. Before you can change, you must be ready and willing. This is the most important challenge you will face on the road to financial freedom. Are you indeed prepared to make a change?

Most people I work with consistently make poor financial decisions that result in debilitating long-term consequences. You may not believe it, but your daily spending habits matter. In my years of experience working with clients of various financial means, I've learned that four factors lead to poor financial decisions, and these are all related to each other: fear of lack, keeping up appearances, financial ignorance, and circle of influence.

1. **FEAR OF LACK**

   I could write an entire book on fear. If you are afraid financially, you will most likely end up suffering instead of thriving. The fear of lack usually stems from unresolved childhood trauma that one tries to avoid. For example, "My parents were broke, but I will never be" may sound like an empowering statement. It can also be true if you grew up in a comfortable household, and your family's fortunes turned for the worse. Everything you need to be financially free is already inside you, but you must push past your fear. Take that leap of faith. In the legendary rap group A Tribe Called Quest's song "Midnight", they say, "Scared money don't make money." Your success is on the other side of fear.

2. **KEEPING UP APPEARANCES**

   The phrase "Keeping up with the Joneses" may seem like an outdated cliché, but maintaining a façade of affluence is even more dangerous thanks to the prevalence of social media as a tool to receive attention. A humorous example, my husband has a friend who endlessly posts his possessions on social media. He will take the most attractive photos of his designer watch while standing next to his luxury car parked outside of the expensive house that he just bought. When I saw the photo he posted, I told my husband, "That's a nice picture, but you know what would make it even nicer? If they removed the weeds from their yard." I know you're probably thinking, *Dang, Nicole, that's harsh,* but I do not believe in faking. Fake and broke are related. That is why each time he posts something, I reply with a laughing emoji. I once asked him if he understood that while the car costs a lot of money, did he have money set aside for his kids to go to college one day? The extra stuff is unnecessary. When you post a lot, you are highlighting a life that does not exist. For too many of us, our priorities are out of order.

3. **FINANCIAL IGNORANCE**

The internet has made everything easily accessible, but a personal education is sometimes needed to achieve financial freedom. Ignorance can be comfortable because it does not force us to ask the tough questions and feel vulnerable. The reality is, ignorance will keep you from achieving your financial mind shift. If you do not know, then ask, read, and learn. When you think you do, ask some more, read some more, and evolve as things change. The one constant thing is change, and in our financial lives, we must adjust, be fluid, and not keep still.

4. **CIRCLE OF INFLUENCE**

In 2017, the movie industry was caught off-guard by the success of a film many considered too genre-specific to be successful. The movie *Girls Trip* featured four black women on an annual trip to attend the Essence Festival in New Orleans. Ryan, Sasha, Lisa, and Dina created a host of unforgettable and insane memories that brought hilarious moments to record movie audiences. I know many enjoyed the film, and yes, I have my girls' trips, too. While we don't do any of the things portrayed in the movie, we know how to have fun.

Each time I go on these trips, I must recognize and prepare myself for the reality that not everyone in my circle of influence has the same relationship with money as I do. Everyone in my circle has a position or a persona when it comes to money. There is the one who is good with money, never had bad credit, and has given us financial advice for years. Then there is the highly-educated friend saddled with student loan and credit card debt. However, she lives beyond her means and loves to stay in luxury hotels on the fanciest beaches. There is another person who wants to be financially free but does not ask for help. Ashamed, she does not want to seem vulnerable in front of her friends. Finally, there is the person who needs to change but is not open to the process. She is the one who shuts down because she is not interested in what we have to say. Some are afraid of admitting to their circle that they need help or are working toward a better financial position. Who are the women in your circle? What is your role in your circle?

I have discovered in my work that these four reasons lead to poor financial decisions. The reality is there are far more that we ignore. The fact is, to make the right decisions, you need a plan and accountability. While tempted to make that purchase because its temporary appeal fascinates you, it is easy to forget your goals. Just because that purchase gives you a pleasurable sensation, it does not mean you need to purchase that Amazon wishlist item or splurge on the chef's menu special. We can be easily seduced while in the moment, but always keep the goal in mind. You are pushing to financial freedom, not temporary satisfaction. It is not easy, but I am here to help.

I developed an On-Demand Financial Genius system that creates a checklist for all your future purchases and impulse buys. There are four questions I advise my clients to ask themselves before any purchases they are unsure about making. If you can answer these questions in a split second, and if you are honest, you may avoid making a regrettable purchase.

Question #1: On a scale from 1-10, how much of a need is this purchase?

Need is a tricky word because our culture has abused and misused it. We *need* new shoes when we already have a dozen pairs. We *need* a new piece of jewelry or accessory to complete our outfit. We *need* to see the latest movie because all our friends are talking about it. You get the point. We do not *need* any of these things; we *want* them. Want is a powerful force but only for those who have no ultimate goals. Want can lead you to purchase extravagant amenities when the basics will do. Want will interfere with you achieving your *90 Days of Forever*. Now, I realize that a scale is subjective for many people.

To some, internal motivation will result in your prioritizing items higher than they should be. True needs are the essentials that you literally cannot survive without. Food, power, transportation, and gas are all essentials that would qualify as a ten on the scale. If the things you are paying for are lower than a nine on the scale, you might need to rethink how much you truly need them in your budget.

Question #2: Does this purchase bring me closer to or further away from my 90 Days of Forever? By how many days, months, or years?

Instead of asking if the purchase will make you look better, ask if it will bring you closer to your ultimate Forever goals. This is the essence of planning with your future in mind. The daily decisions you make either lead you closer or further away from your goal. I highly suggested you actively keep your Forever at the forefront of every major financial decision. Some purchases result in you getting closer to your goals because they create a long-term benefit for you. The purchase could be a new computer to improve your productivity, a journal to track financial plans, or a piece of equipment that will enhance your craft. Any purchases you make outside of your budget will inevitably delay your financial vision.

Question #3: How does this purchase add value to me?

Value is not a cosmetic enhancement that gives you a certain cache when meeting new people or impressing your existing group of friends. Value means you must consider the purchase's actual effect on your life, not just the perceived value. Value is an expression. Do not fall into the trap of exterior enhancement. Keep your values at the center of your purchasing decisions.

To answer this question, you must understand the connection between purchases and expressions of value. The two are directly connected because purchases are expressions of our values. You do not go to Starbucks because the expensive cup of coffee is your only option. You could make a cup of coffee at home in a regular drip coffeemaker. No, the choice to go to Starbucks displays what you value. Maybe you choose that coffee shop because it is close to your job or because your favorite barista works there. You know, the one who makes your special drink exactly the way you like it. For some of us, there is no practical value. We only want to be seen with a Starbucks cup. Because of this reality, that's why this question is so important. If we do not take an honest inventory of what drives us closer or further away from our goal, we will talk ourselves into making purchases that we think enhance us.

Question #4: Is there a more cost-effective option for this purchase?

While food is a necessity, dining out is not essential. You can prepare dinner at home to save money or decide on a cheaper option for your budget's long-term benefit. Choosing the most cost-efficient option when you make daily purchases requires a detailed, long-term plan. You cannot simply fly by the seat of your pants. Your plan must be detailed enough to anticipate hidden costs that can subtract from your budget.

If you scored positively to one or two of these questions, don't do it. It's not worth it. If you scored positively to three of these questions, wait a day to decide or switch an expense out to stay within the same budget. If you scored positively to all four questions, go ahead and make the purchase.

THE LESSON

The first step in your journey to financial freedom is to assess your current relationship with money. Identify the values that may be preventing you from achieving financial freedom. More importantly, focus on your needs and not your wants. Use the questions above to evaluate your purchases. Figure out a method that will help you avoid making impulse buys. For example, if you've saved your credit or debit card on shopping apps such as Amazon, Zappos, Wayfair, etc., remove it. Identify at least three ways that will work to curb your spending.

Play is Built into The Budget

"Shoot for the moon. Even if you miss, you'll land among the stars."

~ Norman Vincent Peale

Most children know what they can safely say around the house and what is off-limits. Violating these rules can get you a swift and sometimes painful punishment. While most kids tiptoed around explicit song lyrics, taking the Lord's name in vain, and speaking certain profane words, I was always nervous my grandmother would catch me saying that dreaded four-letter word—can't. Under no circumstance would my grandmother allow me or my sister to say, "I can't," and saying something was too hard to do would be admonished with a soul-splitting stare from her. My grandmother did not play when it came to that word. We were born into a generational culture of achievement, and there are no acceptable excuses for not being responsible. My grandmother's frustration with negative talk is the biggest influence in my disdain when people say they "can't" do something, and I hear it far more often than you think. Clients are typically overwhelmed by the enormity of their current situation and what it takes to achieve financial freedom. They question whether they can create a life of unlimited freedom and fulfillment. Is it possible?

Some people who walk through the doors of my office have lost the most critical element in their journey toward financial freedom—they have stopped dreaming. The moment you stop dreaming, you are setting yourself up for mediocrity. You have accepted the terms of society and placed an invisible ceiling on your potential to experience true freedom. You have allowed the fear of the unknown to cloud your potential. When you stop dreaming, your 90 Days of Forever can quickly turn into a Forever of Never.

In considering your financial future, you must dream

as big and as expansive as you possibly can. When you stop dreaming, you believe every big thing is ultimately unrealistic. You start to believe the lie that you do not deserve the good things you daydream about while at your 9-to-5 job. Settling is a formula for mediocrity and frustration instead of freedom. You must begin your journey with a larger plan in mind; vow to never hold back when you outline your future.

I tell my clients all the time that play must be built into the budget. Catching a movie at the theatre or taking your dream vacation is not cheap. However, doing these things is possible if you identify them as goals and have a plan to achieve your goal. Whatever you can dream of having is possible, but you must clearly articulate your long-term and short-term goals.

For years, my family budget was tight to the point of obsession. We scraped every penny, limiting what we spent during the week and then splurging a bit on the weekend. Our weekly play was built into the budget and created a sense of anticipation for what adventure lied ahead each weekend. When play is built into your budget, you can truly enjoy it when the time comes. Let me dispel a common myth that my clients often indirectly hint at when they come to my office: Having more *is not* bad.

Creating a financial plan is not meant to restrict your fun and your ability to play. Having a financial plan is merely focusing on your budget to reach your goals of freedom and play. To further drive this point home, I want to introduce you to three people. While they are fictional, their stories are a combination of scenarios that my clients have faced over my many years of financial advising. As you read these stories, see where your story most closely fits in with these three scenarios.

Meet Janet

Janet is a beautiful 25-year-old woman with an active five-year-old son, who is a blessing she received while in college. Her "complicated" relationship with the boy's father prevented them from getting married. Though she is a single mother, Janet is a tireless fighter who is committed to making the best life for her and her son. She worked full-time at a local hardware store, earning just $7.10 per hour without insurance or health benefits. In addition to her meager wages, Janet received food stamps and partial daycare assistance of $180.00 every two weeks. She is a Historically Black College and University (HBCU) graduate with forty thousand dollars of student loan debt. The problem was her current job was not in her chosen major. With a child to care for and a job that only paid minimum wage, she was forced to live in a basement apartment with another friend. Her life was hard, and her financial challenges were even more difficult. Her credit report listed repossessions and extensive debt, and she had nothing to show for it. To top things off, the state served her with a tax lien. When I met Janet, the person who referred her to me was convinced I could help her.

Are you like Janet? Is this scenario similar to your current financial position? Do you feel hopeless like Janet?

Janet's goal: She wanted to be able to afford for her son to take piano lessons and experience special things. She also wanted financial stability that would enable her to travel to exciting places.

Meet Julie

We were neighbors with Julie's family, and despite our cultural differences, we became friends over time. Her husband frequently traveled, leaving her at home while he was away. She did not have a job at the time we met, but she always wanted stuff. And by stuff, I mean STUFF. She was an impulsive spender who was out of control. With her husband's good job, they should have been in a much better financial situation. When we met, under the awkward but hilarious circumstances of new neighbors, she discovered I was a financial expert. She devoted her time to coming over to ask me random questions about finances, and I quickly learned she wanted to work. It may sound crazy, but most people are not built to simply do nothing. She needed a purpose but not just any purpose. Julie wanted to work for herself. She wanted a career that would help the family get out from under the debilitating debt they were currently in from trying to maintain a certain lifestyle.

Can you identify with Julie's situation? Do you have debt from trying to keep up with a lifestyle that your budget cannot afford? Are you striving to work for yourself so you can contribute monetarily to your family?

Julie's goal: To be relevant.

Meet Jerome

In Jerome's situation, making ends meet was not the real problem. He lacked vision and failed to plan. Jerome made a six-figure income as a pilot for a well-known airline. He and his family lived in a million-dollar home that they had not been aggressive in paying off. Also, he and his wife made a series of unwise financial decisions. Jerome worked an exhausting eighty hours per week; he consumed himself with making money. Eventually, pushing himself too hard resulted in him suffering a debilitating heart attack. The family was financially unprepared for this jarring reality and found themselves in financial peril. They had failed to plan and manage their surplus to prepare for unexpected events.

Jerome's goal: He did not want to work an 80-hour workweek. Frankly, he did not want to die.

Although everyone's situation is unique, you may be able to align yourself with some of the circumstances depicted in the scenarios and use the stories to motivate you to do better. Take a moment to write down your profile and discover where you fit into the 90-Day profile. Whether you are in a lower income bracket, middle class, or very wealthy, do not forget to dream.

THE LESSON

We all work hard to provide a living for ourselves and our family. However, we sometimes forget to set aside time and money for rest and recreation. Recreation—whether it is a vacation or a simple day outing—helps bring the family together, and it is our time away from the hustle and bustle of work life. Building play into the budget is just as important as building savings and conquering debt.

Be Decisive!

"Decisiveness is a characteristic of high-performing men and women. Almost any decision is better than no decision at all."
~ Brian Tracy

When I was growing up, my mother always said, "Don't get any credit cards, baby." Being a compliant child, I followed my mother's advice and ran from anything involving credit. I had no idea why I was running from having credit cards because no one never told me why I should not get them. Once I stepped foot on a college campus, I discovered credit cards were easy to obtain. After looking at what the minimum payments would be, I was convinced I could handle it. Ignoring the advice of my mother, I applied for several cards. Like most teenagers, I thought my mother didn't know what she was talking about. *I got this,* I told myself.

After finishing my freshman year, I came home for summer vacation and accidentally left my wallet open one day. Big mistake! When my mother saw the cards, she made me pull each of them out. To her dismay and my shame, I had amassed five thousand dollars in credit card debt in just ten months. In less than one year, I had entered debt. After a swift lecture, my mother worked with me to find the balance owed on each of the cards and then cut them up. I wasn't too fond of her actions at the time, but her doing so saved me from a host of headaches and a world of future financial pain.

While crafting your 90 Days of Forever, you must commit to following the rules. There are some principles in the financial world that you must abide by to experience true financial freedom. Mastering them will save you from making poor financial decisions. Knowing that each of us comes from different backgrounds, I will not comprehensively address every principle, but I will encourage you to apply these to your current financial decision making. These principles, along with the On-Demand Financial Genius, can powerfully shape your financial life and put you on track for your Forever.

PRINCIPLE #1–STAY IN YOUR FINANCIAL LANE

This is an important lesson that most of us do not learn. There are levels of wealth. You must learn to remain on your level and stay in your lane. In his hilarious comedy show, *Laugh at My Pain,* comedian Kevin Hart told the story of hanging out in Las Vegas with one of his friends, who happens to be a famous athlete. His friend offered to pay for everything at the club, but Kevin was too proud to let him. He said, "I got my own money." (He used some other words, but I will keep the book family-friendly.) Unfortunately, Kevin received a bill he was not expecting. While he was able to pay it, he was still uncomfortable with how much money he had to spend on one night of activities.

The next day, the same friend invited him to another gathering. He hilariously talked about why he refused, explaining the dreaded relationship between his checking and savings accounts. "Athletes will mess your life up," he said. Kevin realized at that moment that he was on a different level than his friend. He went on to tell the story of hanging with NBA superstar Dwayne Wade and being pressured to buy a boat. Dwayne has millions of dollars and the financial ability to purchase a boat without a problem. Kevin does not. He made it clear that he has "funny" money, not "boat" money. Kevin's final story is of his friend, actor Mehki Phifer, who invited Kevin's daughter to his son's birthday party at Disneyland. When he arrived, Kevin realized Mehki had bought out the entire park for his son's party. "Now that is real money", Kevin Hart says.

You may not have celebrity friends, but you might have that one friend who constantly pushes your budget to an unsustainable place. You know, that friend who has done well for herself and can go out for drinks every weekend. She should not be your standard. Set your own standard and stay in your financial lane. Here are some questions to ask yourself as a reminder to stay in your lane:

- Am I buying this to keep up with someone else?
- How will my bank account look after this purchase?
- Will this purchase cause long-term hurt for short-term pleasure?
- Am I stepping out of my lane?
- Do my friends have the same financial goals as me?
- What is the maintenance cost?
- How will this purchase impact my household?

Every person must do what is best for them, not their friends.

PRINCIPLE #2–MAKE WISE CREDIT DECISIONS

Many people have similar stories about their experiences with credit cards and how it led to a world of hurt or unwise financial decisions. When we think of credit, we think of low credit scores, high interest rates, past-due accounts, or a dreaded credit card denial. Though most of us have had negative experiences with credit, all credit is not bad.

I want you to understand how to use your credit for your advantage as an investor and not a consumer, but first, I must remind you what is considered good credit. Some people believe they have good credit when in all actuality, their credit is subpar. Here is a helpful standard for understanding your credit score.

Credit Breakdown

- 800+ ~ This score is exceptional and indicates that the borrower is less likely (1%) to become delinquent with their payments.

- 740–799 ~ This score is very good and, like 800+ scores, is above the national average. Only about

2% of borrowers in this range are likely to become delinquent on loans or other types of credit.

- 670–739 ~ This score is good, and the person is considered an acceptable borrower. It means the lender might not offer as low an interest rate as those with higher scores because about 8% of borrowers in this range are likely to become delinquent.

- 580–669 ~ This score is fair but also below the national average. Borrowers in this range will be more likely to pay a higher interest rate than those with better credit since the likelihood of a borrower within this range becoming delinquent with payments is about 28%.

- 579 and lower ~ This score is poor. Borrowers within this range might have to put down a deposit or pay a fee to obtain a credit card or home utility services. About 61% of borrowers in this range are likely to become delinquent.

Credit can be a great thing, but it depends on your uses for it. Consumers think about a good credit score as a prized trophy, thinking they need to protect it. Society has taught us that our credit score is equivalent to our character. So, consumers believe they have to protect their character. That is not why you have good credit, though. Your good credit score is all about using it to purchase an asset that will enhance your life. Your credit score can help you make that big push toward your financial freedom.

I recommend having two separate cards—one for emergencies and the other for everyday purchases. One card should only be used for unexpected occurrences or (God forbid) a tragedy, and the second card set up for day-to-day purchases. Always have two cards for financial stability, and make sure to keep a running tally of your charges, whether on paper or electronically.

PRINCIPLE #3–BE STRATEGIC WITH YOUR LOANS

According to a study done in 2018, most Americans are officially in debt. The study showed that around 80% of baby boomers and Generation X and 82% of millennials owe money in some way. One of the most pressing reasons people have debt in our society is the unfortunate prevalence of loans. Sadly, there is no standard for when or why we apply for a loan. Consumers need to learn to be strategic when applying for a loan.

You should only apply for a loan for large items. A large item is something that appreciates or is over $15,000. Most people need a loan to purchase a car, but we must be careful with how much of a loan we get. Many of the cars that we buy are depreciable assets, causing us to fall into more debt and financial despair. When purchasing a vehicle, try to put down 20% of the total cost up front. Doing so will lower your payments and set you up to be successful in paying it off.

Another study completed in the past decade shows that student loan debt is increasing at a rate of about $2,853 per second. That's a staggering amount of money. Getting a student loan might seem like a good idea at the time, but they can destroy the student's financial future and create a frustrating cycle of constant payments. If you can avoid student loans, by all means, please do. Tell your child to apply for scholarships, work an extra job, take fewer classes, or go to a less expensive school. Parents, set up a college savings plan early, preferably when your child is born. If you have a child who is closer to college-age, have a serious conversation about which schools you can afford to send them. Please do not wait until the child is applying for colleges to inform them of the pool of funds you set aside for them.

These three principles are important in setting the tone for your finances. They keep you grounded and rooted in the pursuit of economic liberation. You must follow the principles to get the ultimate result.

THE LESSON

A commitment to financial freedom requires decisiveness and dedication to goal accomplishment. The decision to travel on the road to financial freedom requires adherence to financial principles and always keeping the goal in mind.

REFLECTION

What are some of your financial principles that I did not mention above? Use the space below to craft your financial Ten Commandments rules that you will not violate to achieve your 90 Days of Forever.

The Devil Is in the Details

"The Warrior of Light pays attention to the small things, because they can severely hamper him."

~ Paulo Coehlo

I have always had great respect for athletes who compete at the highest level. Their push for greatness is inspiring for those of us not blessed with their athletic gifts. While everyone who plays sports at a professional level is incredible, there is another category of athletes. These icons are the most excellent members of their respective sports. Ali, Jordan, Serena, Lebron, Tiger, Kobe, and Bolt are a few who are recognized by just one name. Just like Kevin Durant says, "Hard work beats talent when talent fails to work hard." You have to work every day at your financial stability, making sure that your goals are in line with your spending and lifestyle.

Watching these greats is always fascinating. Not just because they have such incredible physical gifts but because they have a tremendous work ethic. The truly great athletes in sports do not just rest on getting by. They take ownership of their training. One of the greatest boxers of all time hated every minute of preparation, but he wanted to be a champion badly enough to endure the difficulty and follow through for the prize. Ali's quote, "I hated every minute of training, but I said, 'Don't quit. Suffer now and live the rest of your life as a champion." is perfect for summing up your 90 Days of Forever. Experiencing financial freedom is a study in delayed gratification. To experience all the luxury that we deeply desire, we must be committed to a little bit of patience and sacrifice.

I'm sure you don't find old fashioned responsibility to be the most exciting chapter topic. However, the clients who have experienced financial freedom have always taken full responsibility for every money decision they make, including even the smallest purchases. At first, clients may feel like they are suffering and giving unnecessary energy to each transaction. But, in the end, each recognizes that becoming financially free requires taking ownership and making tough choices. To some, it may sound too intangible or slippery to nail down. If I had to put ownership into my own words, I would say that pain plus patience equals true financial ownership.

Pain + Patience = Ownership

Journeying to your 90 Days of Forever is about ensuring you achieve your overall financial goals for your benefit and the advancement of your family. However, if prepared to accomplish your goals, you must endure some pain. One of the first things that I request from my clients after setting a plan is their credit and debit cards. They are often shocked by my boldness to ask for something that they have become so dependent on using. I am forced to do this for some clients because spending has become far too easy for them. They have swiped their cards to pay for unnecessary purchases, leading to financial peril. I must introduce pain, discomfort, and inconvenience.

Removing cards from their wallets or purses forces them to take a few extra steps to get their money. It also forces them to watch the money leave their hands. For most people, this drives home the reality that they are spending too much. For others, they need to receive a daily update alerting them of their bank balance. Waking up to a smaller amount than they expected or seeing how much those subscriptions cost them can be the kick necessary to wake them up to their detrimental spending habits. Still, the reality remains that most of us do not respond to comfort. We need some pain.

I am fully aware you may not have a Nicole Deas with whom you can make an appointment. You can, however, set some pain limits for yourselves. Your pain may be leaving your cards at home every day so that you are not tempted to raid the office café or run to the fast-food restaurant within walking distance of your job. Your pain may be to cancel that vacation you cannot afford or tell your friends that you cannot do drinks this week. Your pain may be saying no to family members and friends when they ask you to pay a bill for them. I have several clients who struggle with refusing when their parents or friends ask them for a loan. Many clients have allowed their family members to use their generosity against them, resulting in their savings withering. As a financial advisor, I believe it is my responsibility to separate your bank account from unhealthy situations. I tell clients to make me the bad guy. Tell whoever is asking for money that Nicole said no. It was hard for some clients, but eventually, using my name was not even necessary. They developed the strength to refuse all on their own.

Pain is all about mustering the courage to say NO. Saying no to yourself or others may feel excruciating, but I guarantee your future self will thank you. Whatever the pain may be to you, you need to step up so you can experience your forever. Think back to Muhammad Ali's quote from early in the chapter. He hated training, but he knew why he was training. Ali knew the pain of training would lead to success in the boxing ring. Try adopting his mentality. Enduring discomfort now will lead to financial freedom and comfort later.

There is Power in Patience

Have you ever been broke? Not the type of financial difficulty where you are unable to purchase designer brands. I am talking about being truly broke to the point where you do not have enough money for your necessities. It is stressful and painful, but the discomfort of having a low bank balance can be motivation never to be in that situation again.

Some of us may have no choice. Life circumstances beyond our control can knock us down completely. However, others do have a choice. We have been blessed to be able to choose not to be in that position any longer. The moment of refusal shapes our commitment to financial patience. Patience is recognizing that whatever delayed the gratification you are experiencing now is better than being saddled with the pain of debt and despair in your future. Patience means you will stick to your plan. It means you will work the plan long enough to ensure it works or adjust it. Patient people can see far beyond their current bank balance and glimpse their Forever.

When I was a young adult, I could not always see this. The latest and greatest things captured my attention, even though I had the upbringing that valued saving and patience. After a few difficulties, I resolved never to be in that place again. I refused to be broke and unprepared for my future. Your budget may take a few days to set up, but do you have the patience to be financially stable? Canceling your streaming subscription may mean that you must wait to catch your favorite show. Do you have the patience to save up so you can experience that dream vacation? Do not let the present keep you from being patient for the future. The future holds your Forever. After you have identified the places that require pain and patience in your budget, you are ready to take ownership. Here are a few principles that will help you determine if you are accepting financial ownership:

Owners have a report card.

A report card is an assessment of how well or poorly you are doing in school. For most of us, receiving our report card struck fear in our hearts when we were kids. We were nervous for our parents to see our report card. That fear is exactly why you need a report card. The question to ask yourself is who or what is holding you accountable to your financial goals. A report card displays what you have done in the past and what you can improve. Your trusted financial advisor or spouse should view your report card. For others, your report card might be an app that tracks your spending, subscriptions, and savings. It would help if you had at least one report card each fiscal quarter.

Owners have a relationship with the word NO.

Every person who is serious about their financial freedom understands how powerful the word NO is to bringing them closer to their goals. When it is time to make a big decision, such as purchasing a car purchase or taking a vacation, you may experience a series of NO's that eventually lead to one YES. The word NO can be powerful in the day-to-day decisions you face about where to eat and what to buy, but it can also be important in major moments. When the holiday season hits, will you exercise discipline or fall prey to the same forces that cause you to overspend every year? When it is time for a birthday or anniversary, will you overspend or exercise a bit more planning and discipline into your special event purchasing? It is essential to plan before every large purchase.

Owners have a comprehensive financial picture.

Ownership means you have a more comprehensive financial picture than just spending and saving. Taking ownership includes having tangible financial benchmarks to achieve your long-term goals.

Here are some things everyone should have:

- Health Insurance
- Life Insurance (Term, Whole, or IUL)
- Savings
- Retirement (401K, IRA, ROTH IRA, Real Estate)
- Long-Term Care Insurance
- Legal Protection or Representation
- Financial Report Card

THE LESSON

Are you prepared for the unexpected? Are you set in case of a family emergency or sudden illness? Do not reduce your comprehensive financial picture to only your spending and saving. Financial freedom is more than that. You need to be prepared for the difficult moments, as well. That is all part of the plan. As we close this chapter on ownership, I want to remind you that you do have what it takes. I know that talking about the nitty-gritty of pain and patience can be uncomfortable and even overwhelming for some of us. However, this is essential to achieving your dreams. Do not look past this crucial step. Instead, embrace it. Take ownership, and you will be closer to your Forever than you would have ever imagined.

REFLECTION

What does financial freedom look like to you? Are you taking ownership of your journey to financial freedom? What are you using as a report card?

What You See Is What You Get

"Too many people spend money they earned....to buy things they do not want...to impress people that they do not like."

~ Will Rogers

It seems like everyone has a favorite money guru with the right formula for achieving your dream situation. They want you to buy their book or financial kit, and then all will be right in your world. Despite their intent, most of these experts make it seem far too easy to accomplish your level of financial freedom. The books or television shows paint a picture that achieving these goals will be, at least, easier than you think it will be or, at worst, a piece of cake. But I am here to burst that bubble.

Let's have a little chat. When I make this comment to my clients, they know they are in for some hard reminders. I love each of my clients too much to let them sit in their misconceptions, so sometimes a little chitchat is necessary. I will share with you the same information that I share with them: You must embrace the process. Most financial shows only share part of this with you, but without this crucial mindset shift of embracing the process, this journey will not be enjoyable or productive for you. The journey to financial freedom is like everything else worth doing—it's difficult. There will be times when you will feel overwhelmed, spent, and ready to throw in the towel. Everyone who has started this journey has faced setbacks. These obstacles can come in the form of comments from others or the mistakes you make. Embrace all these difficulties with open arms.

Part of embracing the process is learning what to do after each crucial step. As I have tried to teach my clients how they should respond to each level of their journey, I find myself constantly repeating a phrase that I believe is crucial to achieving success: Do better next time. Telling someone to do better next time sounds like a reminder for when someone has made a mistake. When you spend too much money on dining out, do better next time.

When you make an impulse purchase and buy a new phone just because it is the latest and greatest, do better next time. Whenever you slip up and make a financial mistake, bounce back and do better. But beyond the negative cognition, do better next time is a rallying cry for you to level up. It is a great way for you to grow and progress past where you are now and do something greater than you did in the past. To do better next time means you can experience far more than you ever imagined, but words are nothing without action.

Even though I tell people to dream big, most tend to aim far lower than they should. They tend to believe that some things are unrealistic or a "pie in the sky" dream. Having this mentality will not help you achieve a satisfying result for your Forever. You will not experience your peak if you do not have high goals and dreams. A few chapters ago, I introduced you to three fictional characters who represent where many of my clients start their journey. Janet, Julie, and Jerome may not fit perfectly into your situation, but they are great examples of where many of us find ourselves. These three individuals come from varied circumstances and have different goals for their Forever. All they needed to hear to progress past their current level was "do better next time".

JANET

Janet wanted her son to have more engaging and memorable experiences than she had as a child. When I asked for her goals, she was focused. She wanted her life to change. She desired to shift from her struggling job to wealth and comfort, and she wanted to take her son to Six Flags or go on a life-changing trip. When she started, her credit score was an abysmal 530, but her goal was clear—she wanted to get her score over 600 by the end of the year. It sounds ambitious, but she was committed to achieving this milestone. For Janet, her "do better next time" goal was to improve her credit score. She felt it would be the beginning of her Forever journey to financial freedom.

Despite her motivation for success, her job environment was frustrating. Her work manager did not believe she was qualified for other positions and made her life extremely difficult. There will always be discouraging voices around you, influencing you to stay where you are so they can easily manage you. These naysayers can drain and discourage you from your goals. When she told me about this situation, it was clear that she was upset by it. I asked what she wanted to do. She had to make an aggressive move. There will be times when you are forced to make a bold move to achieve your goals.

Rather than wrestling with her supervisor, she went above him to the department manager. She asked to discuss upward mobility in the organization with someone in a higher position. Her language was brilliant; she mentioned to the department manager that there were many things she wanted to experience in the company. The manager was impressed, and after researching what was available, he gave her an application to a few different available jobs.

In the meantime, I referred her to résumé writers who would make her job experience even more attractive on paper. After a brief time of preparation, she did not take no for an answer. She applied for every position she could. She wisely stopped pigeonholing herself into what she could and could not do. She stopped worrying about the title of the position and applied for every job that interested her. To her surprise and excitement, she got two jobs in three months. She told me that she was surprised at herself for turning down a job that a few months before she would have jumped at having. She stated the reason she declined the job was because there would be no upward mobility in the department. It wasn't just about finances for her; it was about her confidence and self-esteem. Doing better next time happens from the snowball effect of wins.

Janet planned for her transformation, a decision that she felt most comfortable making. She realized there are always people around you who will influence your money decisions. Whenever Janet visited our office, she would talk about her sister and all the things she was facing with their tense, uncomfortable relationship. She internalized the heavy drama between them, feeling like she was less than because her sister had more money and status than she did. Not only was her sister discouraging, but her mother was also very negative. Janet systematically and psychologically began to remove herself from her toxic environment and dropped people from her circle. She eventually accomplished all her goals. Before then, Janet did not see anything greater than what she had. She stated that I saw something in her that she never saw in herself.

JULIE

Julie was a stay-at-home wife and mother who was simply bored. She was tired of sitting in the house and not pursuing her life goals. Because Julie was my neighbor, I offered her free consultations on the weekend. She was bored sitting at home and wanted to pursue something of her own—she wanted more.

Julie evolved. She went from being a stay-at-home mom to being an entrepreneur. After some consideration, she decided to go into real estate. I must admit that I was a little surprised by that decision, but the bigger surprise came when I saw how she excelled in this field. She was incredible. She went from being a novice to owning and managing eleven properties successfully. Julie was so gifted at real estate that she got bored once again and decided she needed to "do better next time".

What was Julie's better? She decided she wanted a corporate job. When I asked her why, she replied that she had never worked in a corporate setting and wanted a new challenge. Using her experience as a property manager, Julie accomplished her goal and became a successful corporate officer.

If you are passionate about what you are doing, once you reach a plateau, you will seek a higher level. Julie embodies a mindset of determination that I love. She is never satisfied and is now modeling what "doing better next time" looks like to her family and others.

JEROME

For Jerome, it was time for him and his wife to downsize. His 80-hour workweeks as a pilot were severely damaging to his health and well-being—mentally and physically. Therefore, he had to make a change. Their family finally downsized, moving to a more affordable place, and refused to go back to living beyond their means. I was beyond excited for them to free themselves from the pressure to stay in a certain socio-economic class. He knows he can live longer and live comfortably from now on. Furthermore, he knows what comfortable looks like now. He did not want the added stresses of flaunted wealth and power.

Jerome and his family wanted to move downtown, and that's what they did. He is excited about the fact that he has assets and a larger bank account. He talked his wife into living within their means and saving for their future. Now, "doing better next time" looks like retirement.

His mission is to have a comfortable life that he and his wife can continue to enjoy after he leaves his job. Jerome cannot wait to retire and be in a place of satisfaction and rejuvenation. Jerome's forever has changed. His view of retirement has been altered. That is what I call doing better next time.

Do better next time. The point of this important phrase is that you should not be comfortable with where you are presently. Do not remain stagnant and complacent. There is more for you to experience. The 90 Days of Forever journey is all about creating a pattern for progression. Take the steps now that will give you a lifetime of progress and freedom. What you do is not just important for today, but it lays the groundwork for the rest of your life. Do better today so you can do better forever.

REFLECTION

How can you do better next time?

Take Ownership Of the Results

"Money is a guarantee that we may have what we want in the future. Though we need nothing at the moment, it insures the possibility of satisfying a new desire when it arises."

~ *Aristotle*

As a nurse, my mother had flexible working hours. When she pursued her undergraduate degree, her permanent shift was from midnight to 8 A.M. She carried a full-time college schedule and a full-time job. She worked every weekend, which allowed her to have two days off during the week. My mother built her school hours around her children's school hours. When we were in school, she was, too. When we came home, she was there to greet us. After finishing our homework and eating dinner, we would go to my grandma's house to get ready for bed and go to school the next day. This routine lasted a few years. Going to Granny's taught us to be independent. Before leaving for Granny's house, we made sure our books were in our backpacks and our uniforms were pressed. My mother would do the final check before we went. We also learned the importance of time, as my mother needed to return to work at midnight.

Even though she worked the nightshift, summer was always a time for refreshing and recharging. We would visit Riis Beach in Queens, New York, every weekend except for when Granny would take us to Trinidad, West Indies, to visit family. There was freedom in going to the beach, climbing trees, and being in the company of our cousins and other relatives. My sister and I enjoyed the tropical outdoors and learning about the island of our maternal family. Even at a young age, we appreciated the way people in the islands lived. They lived a simple life but seemed to be happy with what they owned. While we were away, our mother focused on graduating sooner by going to summer school. We learned early to appreciate the benefits of hard work and sacrifice. It was beautiful because, from such a young age, my sister and I had a masterclass understanding of how to work hard. But it was not just that. We learned to appreciate why we work hard. The "why" is even more important than the "how".

I did not want to write this book without making it clear that we are not on this journey only because we want to make more money. It is not really about the amount itself at all. It is about what money allows us to experience. Money is temporal, but feelings and lifestyles can change who we are, giving us the happiness and experiences that we need to sustain us. This is why I say peace of mind is the true source of riches.

Don't get me wrong; I'm not saying that having money isn't necessary or that we should not think about how to make it. Money is my job. However, I do recognize that obsessively thinking about money is a waste of time and energy. You will remember different times in your life when you had varying amounts of money, but you will not remember your weekly bank balance. Instead, you will remember the trips you took, the fun you had, and the emotions you felt that were powered by the pursuit of money. Money is just the feeling that drives the vehicle of experiences.

As you start your journey to financial freedom and

your place of ultimate happiness, I want you to remember that you are not here because you want to have a bigger bank account. You are here because you want to experience what true peace of mind looks like in your situation.

What is peace of mind for you? For some, your peace of mind can be expressed within seconds of being asked that question. For others, you are still trying to figure this out. I have some ideas about what peace of mind is for all of us.

Peace of mind feels like rest. In a time when we cannot slow down and do without using our phones for five minutes, rest is elusive. And by rest, I do not mean sleep. Many people are at rest, but they do not have a regular sleep pattern due to their work schedule or unique situation. Peace of mind is the ability to lay down and not worry about what may happen tomorrow. That is rest. In this book focused on financial freedom, I need to remind us that not everyone has the luxury of worrying about their 90 Days of Forever yet. Some people simply need rest, but they cannot rest because they are worried about keeping a roof over their family's head, putting food on the table, and keeping the utilities from being turned off. And let's not think of the horror of running out of gas while in a traffic jam.

They pray daily that nothing unexpected will happen that will drain their already empty bank account and result in getting hit with those dreaded overdraft fees. These people do not want money and riches as much as they want a break from the constant anguish of worry.

Growing up, we knew our granny always had extra for those who needed food. She was known as someone who would always be there for us if we needed any necessities throughout the day or found ourselves in a tough time. My sister and I would marvel at her consistency. Her table always had warm plates and open seats. There was fresh food waiting for us whenever we stopped by. Some people do not have someone who they can go to for hot meals. We were indeed blessed.

I have seen some clients who are doing well financially but cannot seem to shake the feeling of restlessness and anxiety from their lives. For them, they cannot rest because of what they have experienced in their past. Their past of poverty and financial difficulties keep them stuck in the mindset that anything could happen to take their money away. They are paralyzed by the fear of not knowing what tomorrow holds.

Here is a question for you to ponder: *Do your past experiences trigger something within you that causes you to be worried about your future?* After having enough sleepless nights worrying about bills, you likely will still have some worry that resides in your heart and will take a while to leave. You might find yourself constantly checking your bank balance, hoping nothing comes out of the blue and is withdrawn from your account. That worry affects your 90 Days. You cannot go further if you have the weight of anxiety holding you down.

Whatever happened in the past should remain in the past. You may be able to leave the past behind easily and quickly move on, or you may need professional help to put the past behind you. Whichever it is, you deserve better. You deserve rest. You deserve to have peace of mind, whatever that looks like for you. You deserve to be in a place of rest, without worry or concern. Whatever your 90 Days of Forever looks like, it should always include rest.

Peace of mind sounds like laughter. Recently our country was rocked by the death of the legendary fashion designer Kate Spade, the business mogul known for her signature handbags. Her name was synonymous with success and building a fashion empire. Despite all this, Kate tragically took her life. This is why I emphasize that *90 Days of Forever is not just about money in your bank account.* Kate Spade had all the money she could ever want, and still, something was missing from her life.

Without knowing her situation or intimate thoughts, I can say that I have seen far too many people who have external wealth without inner joy. I know millionaires who do not smile even though they could look at their accounts and see millions of reasons to smile. Are you happy? The 90 Days of Forever journey requires you to seek your happiness, not anyone else's idea of what you should or should not do. It requires you to be able to laugh. Ask yourself this: *How often do you laugh?*

My favorite memories growing up almost always involve side-splitting laughter. We tell jokes and stories from our childhood. I am most happy about the fact that I can laugh in the present, as well. My family makes it a point to incorporate laughter into our daily lives because those who are truly rich are the ones who smile and laugh.

The clients who have taken great strides are the ones who come out being funnier after their journey. Remember Jerome? He was once such a serious man, but now that guy has jokes all the time. He is always laughing and clowning with his family because he realizes he now has the freedom and energy to do so. Whatever your goal is, it should include laughter.

Peace of mind looks like legacy. Writing this book was an interesting experience because it required me to think about my children. Children are one of life's greatest blessings, but kids grow up in the blink of an eye. Every age brings with it financial challenges that can cause you and your family stress. Beyond the immediate concerns, we must think about our kids' future.

As parents, we want to provide our children the opportunity to attend the best schools, have sufficient healthcare coverage, and create memorable life experiences. We want them to dream as large as their heart desires without having to worry about paying for it. As I think about my Forever, it will always involve my children.

Whether or not you are a parent, you should consider your legacy. How will you leave the world better than before you came into it? What will you leave behind that can remain long after you are gone? Too many people have lower standards for themselves because they do not believe they will ever have anything to pass down. Even if you do not have children or immediate family, you can still pass your legacy down to others and make their lives better.

Here's something to ponder on this journey: *Do you have a plan to better the lives of others around you?* What is your plan to create a legacy that lives on after you pass away? The greatest people in society do not have to be the richest, but they will have made the most impact on others. Every client who I have ever spoken to about this journey has mentioned a child, a parent, a friend, a spouse, or someone they love that they are inspired by and want to encourage through their journey. It's not just about you. Your Forever goal should also change someone else's life.

Peace of mind is the true source of riches. Peace of mind feels like relief. Peace of mind feels like joy. Peace of mind looks like leaving a legacy for others around you. I hope this journey is not just one about money and belongings. I hope this journey is truly about intangibles. Do not let money be your joy. Let money *fuel* your joy!

Conclusion

Some of the principles found in this book may appear to be drastic or too radical for you, but I need you to understand that your goals *are* attainable. You can reach the highest point of your financial dreams if you follow the principles outlined in this book and commit yourself to your written goals.

Now, before you put this book down and rush to start your journey, I must prepare you for what you will face. At times, it will be difficult, draining, and drastic. You will be challenged to account for every penny of your budget and make serious, necessary decisions about the future of you and your family. You will be required to take a deep, inward look at the person you want to become and commit yourself to that vision. You may even come to the point where you need to clarify your relationships with family and friends who may be distracting you from your Forever goal.

When I ask my clients what their journey feels like, you might think they would be quick to voice how difficult, draining, or drastic the process is for them. However, the first thing they mention is freedom. While challenging, your mind shift towards your Forever will also be a time of brilliant discovery. You will find yourself feeling freer and more secure than ever before. You will discover that you can accomplish goals that previously seemed unattainable. You will also find that your finances are in a much healthier place.

Remember Janet? Her journey brought her the unforgettable experience of taking her son to a beautiful amusement park. Janet thought she could not get out of her minimum wage job, but she is now in a place to decide what she wants to do next. She could start a business, be a corporate executive for a successful company, travel the world with her son, and even more than she ever imagined. Janet's journey took her there.

Remember Julie? She went from being a woman who was bored and unfulfilled, to a corporate titan able to command the respect of her colleagues who thought they were more experienced than her. She conquered that corporate space and then became the owner of eleven properties as a real estate broker simply because she worked to achieve it. Julie's journey took her there.

Remember Jerome? He went from working 80-hour weeks, exhausting himself to the point that he had a heart attack. He tried to maintain a certain standard of living for him and his wife, only for his efforts to almost end up killing him. When he started his journey, he had a different standard of success, but he has finally become a free and healthy man. Jerome's journey took him there.

As your journey progresses, you will have a new outlook on what it means to be whole and healthy. You will find yourself at a place where you can breathe, think, and dream. Remember, you are not doing this for a short-term challenge. You are doing this for your Forever.

You cannot approach your 90 Days of Forever with the same mindset and approach you had when you first started reading this book. You cannot continue to do the same thing and expect different results. As the adage says, "If you always do what you've always done, you will always get what you've always gotten." Nothing about this journey should be ordinary.

The first part of your Forever sets the stage for stability, but the next will set the stage for abundance. The following activities will help you envision your future destiny. This list is not exhaustive, but it will help you to create a mindset and vision of where you want to see your life in the future.

1. **Vision Board**
   Open your Pinterest app, purchase a poster board, or pull out an old-fashioned notebook and compile some pictures. You must be able to see where you are currently to plan where you are going. Include pictures of your dream house, dream car, and maybe even your dream job if you do not already have it. The more pictures you place on your board, the better.

2. **Write a Vacation Wishlist**
   Going on a vacation is one thing, but experiencing a limitless vacation is something altogether different. Presently, you may not be able to afford the tickets, parking, refreshments, souvenirs, and other expenses involved with visiting a popular amusement park. Currently, your finances may only allow you to go on a 4-day cruise instead of a 14-day expedition. Whatever your dream vacation is, create the wishlist you desire to experience. It will ensure you never have another boring trip.

3. **Budget Your Budget**
   After reading this book and taking action, you will have already budgeted your finances. Your budget, however, will need to be adjusted periodically. That's because as your money increases, you will have to take the time to reconfigure your simple money goals. Should you spend more or less than previously on amenities or desires? You must become creative and disciplined to accomplish your Forever goals.

4. **Dream for Your Family**
   When you started your journey, naturally, you were considering yourself, your finances, and your dreams. But we must look beyond ourselves to continue the journey toward true happiness and freedom. Whether for your partner, spouse, or children, you can leave someone you love a legacy. Perhaps your journey will become all about them, or maybe it will be about giving back to others who helped to create your success.

If you discovered you had 90 days left to live on this earth, what would you do and with whom? Why? I am asking you to consider answering these questions truthfully. Let this book be a springboard to aggressively pursuing your journey toward financial freedom. That is all I am asking you to do. Do you want to experience financial freedom, peace of mind, and fulfill your dream? You may slip and fall during the journey, but get up, dust yourself off, and continue moving forward. Do not delay. Your forever awaits you.

Glossary

Compound Interest

When you're investing or saving, this is the interest you earn on the amount you deposit, plus any interest you've accumulated over time. When borrowing, the interest is charged on the original loan and the interest charges that accrue against your outstanding balance over time. Think of it as "interest on interest." It will make your savings or debt grow faster than simple interest, which is calculated on the principal amount alone.

FICO Score

A number used by banks and other financial institutions to measure a borrower's creditworthiness. FICO is an acronym for the Fair Isaac Corporation. This company came up with the methodology for calculating a credit score based on several factors, including payment history, length of credit history, and the total amount of debt owed. FICO scores range from 300 to 850. The higher the score, the better the terms you may receive on your next loan or credit card. People with scores below 650 may have a harder time securing credit at a favorable interest rate.

Net Worth

The difference between your assets and liabilities. You can calculate your net worth by adding up all the money or investments you have, including the current market value of your home and car, as well as the balances in any checking, savings, retirement, or other investment accounts. Then subtract all of your debt, including your mortgage balance, credit card balances, and any other loans or obligations. The resulting net worth number helps you take the pulse on your overall financial health.

Investing Terms

Asset Allocation

The process by which you choose what proportion of your portfolio you'd like to dedicate to various asset classes based on your goals, personal risk tolerance, and time horizon. Stocks, bonds, and cash or cash alternatives (like certificates of deposit) make up the three major types of asset classes. Each of these reacts differently to market cycles and economic conditions. For instance, stocks have the potential to provide growth over time but may also be more volatile. Bonds tend to have slower growth but are generally perceived to have less risk. A common investment strategy is to diversify your portfolio across multiple asset classes to spread out risk while taking advantage of growth.

Bonds

Commonly referred to as fixed-income securities, bonds are essentially investments in debt. When you buy a bond, you're lending money to an entity, typically the government or a corporation, for a specified period at a fixed interest rate (also called a coupon). Then, you receive periodic interest payments over time and get back the loaned amount at the bond's maturity date. Bond prices tend to move in the opposite direction of interest rates—that is, when interest rates rise, bond prices typically fall.

Capital Gains

The increase in the value of an asset or investment—like real estate or stock—above its original purchase price. The gain, however, is only on paper until sold. A capital loss, by contrast, is a decrease in the asset's or investment's value.

Rebalancing

The process of buying or selling investments over time to maintain your desired asset allocation. For example, if your target allocation is 60% stocks, 20% bonds, and 20% cash, and the stock market has performed particularly well over the past year, your allocation may now have shifted to 70% stocks, 10% bonds, and 20% cash. If you wanted to return to that 60/20/20 asset allocation, you'd have to sell some stocks and buy some bonds.

Stocks

Also called equities or shares, stocks give you ownership in a company. When you buy stocks, you become a company shareholder, giving you claim to part of that company's assets and earnings.

Real Estate Terms

Adjustable-Rate Mortgage (ARM)

A type of mortgage in which the interest you pay on your outstanding balance rises and falls based on how interest rates are changing in the larger market. ARMs usually start at a fixed rate for a short period and then reset annually.

Amortization

The process of paying off your debt in regular installments over a fixed period. Your mortgage is amortized using monthly payments that are calculated based on the amount borrowed and the interest you would pay over the life of the loan.

Escrow

An account held by an impartial third party on behalf of two parties in a transaction. During the home-buying process, the buyer will deposit a specified amount in an escrow account that neither party can access until the terms of the purchase contract, such as passing an inspection, have been fulfilled and the sale completed. An escrow account can also hold money later used to pay your homeowners insurance and property taxes. You can put money in escrow every month so when your premiums and taxes are due, you have enough to cover those bills.

Fixed-Rate Mortgage

A fixed-rate mortgage is a mortgage that carries a fixed interest rate for the entire life of the loan. With a fixed-rate mortgage, the amount of your payment does not increase if interest rates rise. The downside is you could be locked into a more expensive mortgage if interest rates go down.

Private Mortgage Insurance (PMI)
A type of insurance that mortgage lenders require when homebuyers provide a down payment of typically less than 20%. The premiums are usually tacked onto the amount homeowners pay each month. For some mortgages, once your loan-to-value ratio reaches 80%, you no longer have to pay PMI, but in some cases, it is permanent for the life of the loan.

Job Benefits Terms

Defined-Benefit Plans
Employer-sponsored retirement plans, such as pensions, in which the employer promises a specified retirement benefit based on a formula that may include an employee's earnings history, length of employment, and age. The employee may or may not be required to contribute to the plan. Because of their high costs, many companies no longer offer this type of benefit.

Defined-Contribution Plans
A retirement plan companies may offer as a job benefit,

which lets employees contribute their own money into an account for retirement. The employer may also choose to match a certain amount of those contributions. The 401(k) and 403(b) are the most common forms of defined-contribution plans. The money that goes into these accounts also typically provides a tax benefit, as long as you don't make withdrawals before retirement age (age 59½ or older).

Executive Compensation

This pay and benefits package provided to senior executives is usually different from what is offered to the typical employee. Executive compensation often includes a base salary, bonuses, incentives based on the company's earnings (such as stock options), income guarantees in the event of a sale or public stock offering, and a guaranteed severance package. These packages are typically negotiated individually and spelled out in employment contracts.

Insurance Terms

Permanent Life Insurance

A policy that provides coverage over the lifetime of the insured. It also offers a component called "cash value" that you can tap into while you're still alive. Using the cash value, however, means you could reduce your death benefit and may owe taxes. Premiums for permanent life insurance are typically more expensive than for term life insurance.

Premium

The payments you make to an insurance company to maintain your coverage. Premiums may be paid monthly, quarterly, semiannually, or annually.

Term Life Insurance

A policy that provides coverage over a set period, generally anywhere from 10 to 30 years. If you die within the set term, your beneficiaries receive a payout. If you don't, the policy expires with no value.

Tax-Related Terms

Adjusted Gross Income (AGI)

Your AGI is calculated as your gross income (e.g., what you earn from your job, a pension, or from interest on investments) minus certain IRS-specified deductions. You calculate your AGI Form 1040 when you file your taxes. Your AGI serves as the basis for determining your taxable income and whether you qualify for certain credits or deductions.

Dependent
A person who is financially dependent on your income, typically a child or an adult relative you support. You may be able to claim certain tax credits or deductions for these dependents on your taxes.

Itemized Deduction
A qualified expense that the IRS allows you to subtract from your AGI that helps further reduce your taxable income. Itemized deductions can include mortgage interest, medical and dental costs, or gifts to charity. Itemized deductions must be noted on IRS form Schedule A.

Standard Deduction
A standard amount used to reduce your taxable income should you decide not to itemize your deductions. Your standard deduction is based on your tax-filing status, and it's the government's way of ensuring that at least some of your income is not subject to tax.

Appendix

Reference Materials

- https://www.solereview.com/what-does-it-cost-to-make-a-running-shoe
- Board of Governors – The Federal Reserve System: Report on the Economic Well-Being of U.S. Households in 2017 – May 2018 - https://www.federalreserve.gov/publications/report-economic-well-being-us-households.htm
- http://money.com/money/4168510/why-student-loan- crisis-is-worse-than-people-think/

Books Referenced

- Tony Robbins - *Money Master the Game: 7 Simple Steps to Financial Freedom*
- Ayn Rand - *Atlas Shrugged,* Mass Market Paperback
- Lao Tzu – *The Way of Life, According to Laotzu*
- Norman Vincent Peale – *The Power of Positive Thinking*
- Paulo Coehlo - *Warrior of the Light: A Manual*

Financial Websites

- www.asktrim.com
- www.truebill.com
- www.acorns.com
- www.stashinvest.com

Credit Apps

- https://www.creditsesame.com/myfreecreditscore
- www.mint.com

About the Author

Nicole L. Deas, MBA, AAMS, CFEI, is the founder and lead advisor of One Source Financial Solutions. She serves as a Wealth Strategist, Licensed Insurance Agent, and Certified Financial Education Instructor.

Prior to founding her advisory firm, Nicole assisted on the trading floor at Wachovia Bank (now Wells Fargo). She was trained to assist corporate and individual clients with identifying investment and insurance services that would help them achieve their financial goals. Earlier, Nicole interned with Citigroup in New York, where she was responsible for analyzing mathematical models of interest rates and market fluctuation for making better portfolio decisions.

With over 25 years within the financial and life insurance industries, Nicole is known for her business acumen, strategic perspective, operational execution, collaborative leadership style, and appetite for taking on new challenges. She holds a bachelor's degree in Policy Studies and Business Administration from Syracuse University, an MBA from Southern Polytechnic State

University, and holds life and health insurance licensure in 20 states. She is also the author of her best-selling book, *90 Days of Forever*.

She has secured her Accredited Asset Management Specialist certification from The College for Financial Planning and is a Certified Financial Education Instructor with the National Financial Educators Council.

Nicole is a member of the Financial Planning Association (FPA), The National Association of Insurance and Financial Advisors (NAIFA), the Cobb Chamber of Commerce, Acworth and Kennesaw Business Association, and a member of Zeta Phi Beta Sorority, Inc. She also sits on the board of the Zeal Foundation of Georgia, serving underprivileged women and children.

Nicole is the loving wife to Darrin Deas and the mother of two beautiful children, Imani and Kanye. She loves active sports, including hang gliding, bungee jumping, parasailing, skydiving, and all water sports.

CPSIA information can be obtained
at www.ICGtesting.com
Printed in the USA
LVHW011711250620
658900LV00020B/2300

9 781734 827880